Countries of the World

South Africa

by Michael Dahl

Content Consultant:
Ezra Mtshonshi
Embassy of the Republic of South Africa

Bridgestone Books
an imprint of Capstone Press

Bridgestone Books are published by Capstone Press
818 North Willow Street, Mankato, Minnesota 56001
http://www.capstone-press.com

Library of Congress Cataloging-in-Publication Data
Dahl, Michael S.
      South Africa/by Michael Dahl.
      p. cm.--(Countries of the world)
      Includes bibliographical references and index.
      Summary: Discusses the history, landscape, people, animals, food, sports, and culture
of the country of South Africa.
      ISBN 1-56065-739-1 (alk. paper)
      1. South Africa--Juvenile literature. [1. South Africa.]
I. Title. II. Series: Countries of the world (Mankato, Minn.)
DT1719.D34   1998
968--dc21
                                                    97-44467
                                                    CIP
                                                    AC

Editorial credits:
Editor, Christy Steele; cover design, Timothy Halldin; interior graphics, James Franklin;
   photo research, Michelle L. Norstad

Photo credits:
Brian Beck, cover, 12
Capstone Press, 5 (left)
Betty Crowell, 8, 20
Root Resources/John Hoellen, 6; Grmkuze, 14
South Africa Tourist Board, 5 (right), 16
Unicorn Stock Photos/A. Ramey, 10, 18

Table of Contents

Fast Facts

Name: Republic of South Africa
Capitals: Cape Town, Pretoria, Bloemfontein
Population: More than 41 million
Main Languages: Afrikaans, English
Religions: Christian, Muslim, Hindu

Size: 470,689 square miles
  (1,223,791 square kilometers)
South Africa is 12 times larger than the U.S. state of Illinois.
Crops: Corn, grains, potatoes

Maps

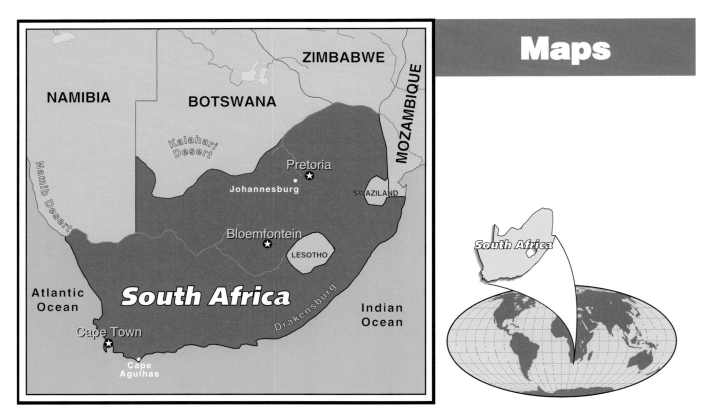

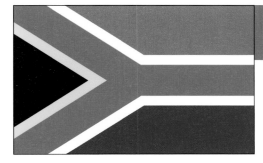

Flag

South Africa's flag is made up of many different colors. White stands for peace. Gold stands for the wealth of South Africa's land. Green stands for South Africa's plants and crops. Blue stands for the sky. Black stands for South Africa's native people. Red stands for people who have died fighting for freedom.

Currency

The unit of currency in South Africa is the rand.

About four rands equal one U.S. dollar.

The Land of South Africa

South Africa covers the southern tip of Africa. It is one of the largest countries in Africa. It is divided into nine parts called provinces.

South Africa touches two oceans. The Indian Ocean is on its east side. The Atlantic Ocean is on its west side. The two oceans meet at Cape Agulhas (uh-GU-luhs). Cape Agulhas is the most southern point in all of Africa.

There is a rocky plateau in the center of South Africa. A plateau is an area of high, flat land. The Namib (NAHM-ib) and Kalahari (Kah-luh-HAH-ree) Deserts are north of the plateau. South of the plateau are huge cliffs and mountains.

Years ago, Dutch settlers moved to South Africa. They called themselves Afrikaners (Af-ruh-KAH-nurz). They created a new language called Afrikaans. The Afrikaners mined diamonds and gold hidden beneath the mountains.

South Africa touches two oceans.

Apartheid

Black Africans were the first people to live in South Africa. They lived in large groups called tribes. Some still live in tribes. Each tribe has its own language, clothing, and way of life. The Zulu (ZOO-loo) tribe is the largest in South Africa.

Other European settlers came after the Afrikaners. European settlers had their own way of doing things. Many of the white and black South Africans did not get along.

The white South African government made apartheid laws. Apartheid is the practice of keeping people of different races apart. People who broke these laws were put in jail. Many people worked for a long time to change the laws.

The government finally made new laws. These laws gave black and white South Africans equal rights. A right is something the law allows people to do. In 1994, Nelson Mandela became South Africa's first black president.

Black Africans were the first to live in South Africa.

Going to School

During apartheid, black and white children attended different schools. Since 1993, all children attend school together.

Children from age seven to 16 must attend school. School is free for all South Africans. Most students must wear uniforms.

There are many languages in South Africa. Children are taught in their own language. They also study English or Afrikaans.

Students study math, history, and science. They can also learn music. Many students join clubs that meet after school. Children can join music, art, or sports clubs.

City schools are often better than schools in the country. South Africa is working to change this. The government is building new schools and training new teachers.

Children of all races now attend school together.

South African Food

People in the city buy food from grocery stores. People in the country often buy food from outdoor markets.

Corn is an important part of South African food. Putu (POO-too) is a favorite food made from corn. Putu is a thick cereal.

Some South Africans have a weekly cookout called a braii (BRY). Mutton is a popular food at braiis. Mutton is meat made from sheep. Karoo mutton has a sweet flavor. This flavor comes from sweet desert plants that some sheep eat.

South Africans also eat biltongs. A biltong is a dried strip of meat. The most popular biltong comes from the kudu (KOO-doo) antelope. Antelope meat is also called venison. People often eat venison for dinner.

People in the country buy food from outdoor markets.

Animals in South Africa

Many people visit South Africa to go on safaris. A safari is a trip taken to see wild animals. Some animals live only in South Africa. Two of these animals are the black rhinoceros and the Cape Mountain zebra.

South Africa has many national parks and preserves. A preserve is a place where hunters cannot kill animals. Preserves protect lions, elephants, giraffes, and ostriches from hunters.

More than 20 kinds of antelope live in South Africa. The Suni (SOO-nee) is the smallest antelope. It grows only 14 inches (36 centimeters) tall.

South Africa's trees and grasslands are full of unusual birds. The gompou (GOM-poo) is the heaviest bird that can fly. A gompou can weigh up to 45 pounds (20 kilograms). The sunbird lives only in South Africa. The sunbird sips nectar. Nectar is a sap found in flowers.

Preserves protect giraffes and other animals.

Cities

Most people in South Africa live in large cities. Pretoria is one of South Africa's capital cities. It is also called Jacaranda City. This is because city streets are lined with jacaranda (jak-uh-RAN-duh) trees. In October, the trees grow bright purple flowers.

Johannesburg is the largest city in South Africa. It is a modern city with many glass skyscrapers. Johannesburg has many museums, parks, stores, and office buildings. It also has many businesses. People move to Johannesburg to find jobs.

Soweto is a town within Johannesburg. Soweto is a shortened name for Southwest Township. Soweto was a black township during apartheid. Black South Africans could not leave the town after dark. Now, many black South Africans have moved from Soweto into Johannesburg.

Jacaranda trees line the streets of Pretoria.

South African Sports

Rugby and association football are the most popular sports in South Africa. Rugby is a form of football. Association football is called soccer in North America.

Many South Africans play basketball. People also enjoy tennis, golf, and cricket. Cricket is a game like baseball. It is played with wide, flat bats and small balls.

Some South Africans play polo. Polo is a game played on horseback by two teams. The players use long wooden clubs to hit a ball. South Africa has a 2,700-mile (4,347- kilometer) coastline with many beaches. South Africans and visitors take part in water sports. They enjoy swimming and fishing. Penguins swim with people along some Cape Town beaches.

Other people snow ski in the Drakensberg Mountains. South Africa is the only African country with snow-covered mountains.

Cricket is played with wide, flat bats.

Holidays

Many South Africans celebrate the same holidays as North Americans. Celebrate means to do something enjoyable on a special occasion. New Year's Day, Easter, and Christmas are all South African holidays.

Music is an important part of South African holidays. Some black South Africans practice their tribe's traditions. A tradition is a custom practiced for many years. They perform traditional songs and dances on holidays, birthdays, and weddings.

Every spring, many people attend the Splashy Fen Music Festival. It is held at the foot of the Drakensberg Mountains. Local singers, choirs, and rock musicians perform.

Some tribe members perform traditional dances.

Hands On: Play Count and Cover

Count and Cover is a game many South African children play. You can play a form of the game.

What You Need

One die   Sheets of paper
Pencils   Buttons or small coins

What You Do

1. Give each player a piece of paper and a pencil. Ask the players to write the numbers one through six on their sheets of paper.
2. Choose one player to go first. Have this player roll the die. See what number the die shows. Have this player cover the number on his or her paper. The player should cover the number with a button or coin.
3. Take turns rolling the die. Each player rolls only once during each turn.
4. The winner is the first person to cover all six numbers.

Learn to Speak Afrikaans

good morning	goeie more	(HOO-eh MOR-eh)
good night	goeienag	(HOO-eh-nah)
how are you?	howzit?	(HOW-zit)
no	nee	(NEE)
please	asebblif	(AHS-uh-bleef)
thank you	dankie	(DAHNK-uh)
what?	wat?	(FAHT)
when?	waneer?	(fah-NEER)
yes	ja	(YAH)

Words to Know

Afrikaners (Af-ruh-KAH-nurz)—relatives of the first Dutch people who settled in South Africa

apartheid (uh-PART-hate)—the practice of keeping people of different races apart

plateau (pla-TOH)—an area of high, flat land

preserve (pri-ZURV)—a place where hunters cannot kill animals

putu (POO-too)—a thick cereal made from corn

tribe (TRIBE)—a group of people who share the same language and way of life

Read More

Flint, David. *South Africa.* Austin, Tex.: Raintree Steck-Vaughn, 1997.

Heinrichs, Ann. *South Africa.* New York: Children's Press, 1997.

Useful Addresses and Internet Sites

**Embassy of the Republic
of South Africa**
3051 Massachusetts Avenue NW
Washington, DC 20008

South African Tourist Board
500 Fifth Avenue
New York, NY 10110

South Africa—Discover a Vast and Varied Land
http://rodie.animal.uiuc.edu/Documents/RSA.html

South Africa in Cyberspace
http://www.geocities.com/TheTropics/8240

Index